NEW WORDS, NEW FRIENDS

Karen Nemeth and Diego Jiménez Manzano

Evidence-based strategies to help children with different languages learn to play together!

KN

Special thanks to Leah J. Mullen for constructive editing and design consultation.
Thank you to Matthew Mullen for editing assistance.
Thank you to Gerardo Lazaro for Spanish translation.

DJM

Special thanks to my family.
I wish to dedicate this book to my father, Antonio.

Language Castle Press
PO Box 883
Newtown, PA 18940
LanguageCastlePress@gmail.com

ISBN: 978-0-9899899-0-9

NEW WORDS, NEW FRIENDS

Karen Nemeth and Diego Jiménez Manzano

"My name is Theo!"
"My name is Wyatt!
I've got a kite –
do you want to help fly it?"

Theo and Wyatt
became friends that day.
They got together
to share and play.

On the first day of school
the boys started a game.
"Let's throw the ball to
whomever we name!"

Wyatt said "Theo!"
and threw the ball hard.
It went over Theo's head
and out to the yard.

The New Kid got the ball
and bounced it away.
"Hey, You!" cried the boys,
"we need the ball to play!"

"Why won't she share?",
they asked teacher Nan.

"Maybe she's doing the best
that she can!"

"Our new friend is speaking
a language we don't.

So , if you ask her to share ,
she probably won't."

"When a friend speaks a language that's different to you

these are three things you can easily do."

1 is:

speak slowly -

clear and clean.

Your new friend's just learning what our words **mean**

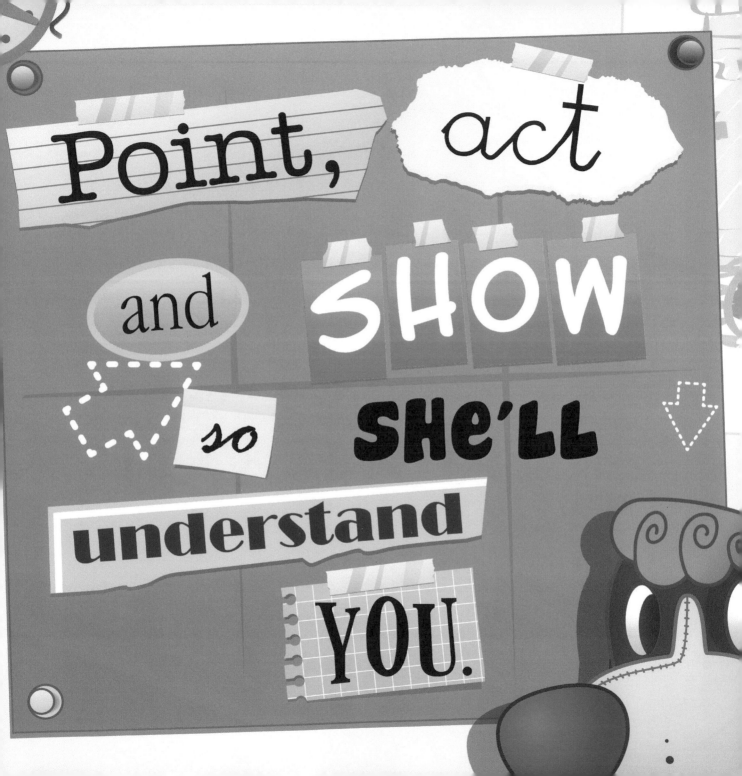

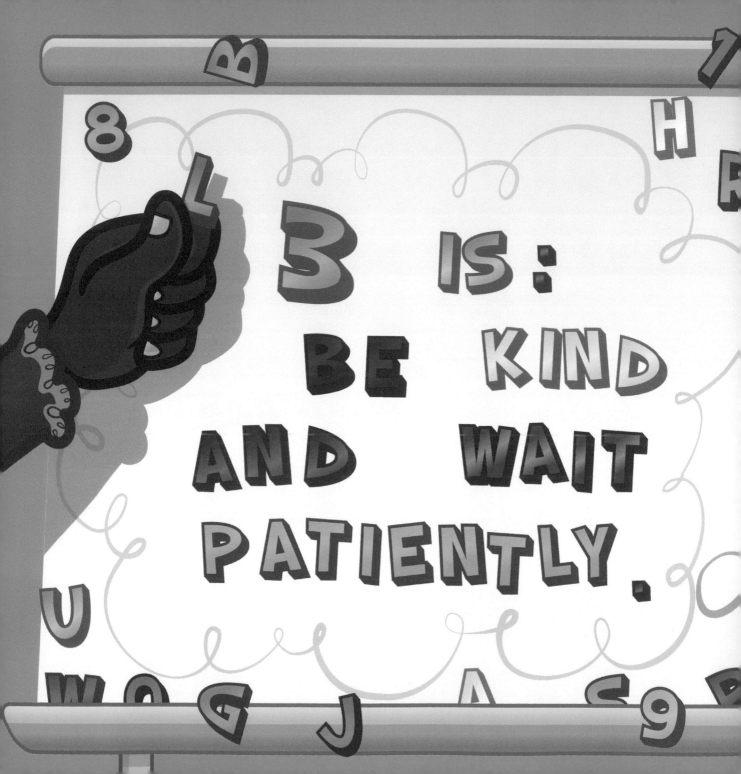

Now let's start by saying
our names out loud.

Hearing our name
makes us
pleased and proud.

To say a friend's name
is the best thing to do.

It's better by far than yelling,
"Hey You!"

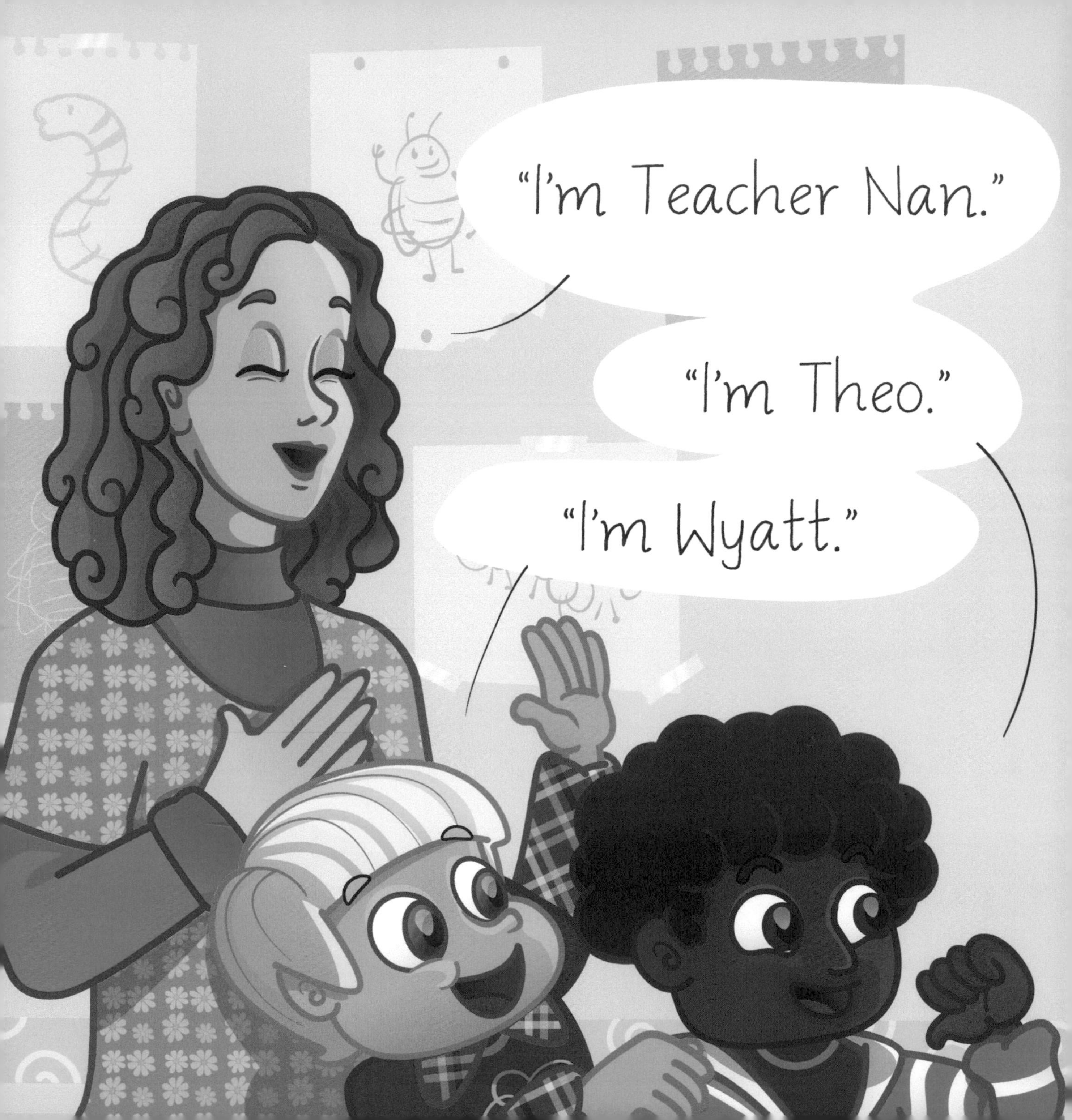

"I'm Teacher Nan."
"I'm Theo."
"I'm Wyatt."

The New Kid
looked shy and said,

"My name ... Violet!"

"Let's run ... Violet ...
Let's RUN ," Theo said.

The three new friends
ran around the flower bed.

"Let's paint ," said Wyatt as he showed her the brush.

She gave him a smile and joined in with a rush.

"Let's share ," said the boys then they waited patiently. Violet saw their kind eyes and joined in happily.

Violet wanted to play
a new ball-bouncing
game.

She showed her
friends how and they
did the same.

Theo, Wyatt and Violet
had all learned a lot.
Was it hard to communicate?
No it was NOT!

"Your ideas worked!"
Theo told Teacher Nan.
"We can share and play
together! Really we can!"

SHARE

Soon the three children
spoke words old and new

Now there are three friends
where once there were two!

FRIENDS

LOVE

Discussion Questions

to get children talking about the ideas in the story

1 To say a friend's _____ is the best thing to do. What is the best thing to do? (Call our friends by their names.)

2 What happened in the story when the New Kid got the ? (she went off and played by herself.)

Wyatt

3 What happened in the story when took the time to show his new friend about the paint brush? (Violet understood that he wanted to share with her and she was able to join in painting.)

4 How did the boys feel when the New Kid took their ?

Violet

5 How did  feel when she didn't have anyone to play with?

6 What do  and do together that helps them be friends?

7 Why is it important to speak slowly and clearly to new friends? (When we speak slowly and clearly, we help people who are new to our language to make sense of what we say.)

8 How does it help when we point, act and show a new friend what we want them to know? (Using gestures and demonstrating help us communicate with other people who don't understand our words.)

9 Why does it help to wait patiently for a new friend to understand us? (waiting patiently helps a newcomer to have time to think and understand what we are saying to them and what they want to say to us – it may take them longer than it takes us when we are speaking our own language.)

10 How do you feel when someone doesn't understand you? Has that ever happened to you? What did you do about it?